THIS BOO

Name:	Age:

Favourite player:

2017-2018

My Predictions...   Actual...

Forest's final position:

Forest's top scorer:

Championship winners:

Championship top scorer:

FA Cup winners:

EFL Cup winners:

Contributors: Rob Mason & Peter Rogers

A TWOCAN PUBLICATION

©2017. Published by twocan under licence from Nottingham Forest FC.

ISBN: 978-1-911502-33-3

PICTURE CREDITS: Action Images, Press Association, Rex by Shutterstock.

£9

C000138281

CONTENTS

Eric
LICHAJ | 02

POSITION: Defender **NATIONALITY:** American **DOB:** 17.11.1988

DID YOU KNOW? The USA international full-back's passionate performances have ensured that Eric is a firm favourite with fans and teammates alike, earning him last season's Player of the Season award.

Michael
MANCIENNE | 04

POSITION: Defender **NATIONALITY:** English **DOB:** 08.01.1988

DID YOU KNOW? Michael started his professional career at Chelsea and played in the Champions League in 2008-09, coming on as a substitute for Michael Ballack in a 1-0 win against Juventus at Stamford Bridge.

Matt MILLS | 05

POSITION: Defender **NATIONALITY:** English **DOB:** 14.07.1986

DID YOU KNOW? As a youngster, Matt was originally a central midfielder when he was with Swindon Town's centre of excellence, before his move to Southampton where he was converted to a centre-back by one of the coaches.

Armand TRAORE | 06

POSITION: Defender **NATIONALITY:** Senegalese **DOB:** 08.10.1989

DID YOU KNOW? Former Arsenal defender Armand Traore represented France at both Under 19 and Under 21 level before opting to play international football for his parents' native country Senegal, going on to pick up five caps.

Liam BRIDCUTT | 07

POSITION: Midfielder **NATIONALITY:** English **DOB:** 08.05.1989

DID YOU KNOW? Despite being born in Reading in Berkshire, Liam has made two appearances for Scotland, qualifying through his Edinburgh-born grandfather, and made his international debut against Serbia in March 2013.

Chris COHEN | 08

| POSITION: | Midfielder | NATIONALITY: | English | DOB: | 05.03.1987 |

DID YOU KNOW? A very popular figure among supporters for his passion for Nottingham Forest on and off the pitch, Chris has made more than 300 appearances in the Garibaldi since joining the club from Yeovil Town in 2007.

Daryl MURPHY | 09

| POSITION: | Forward | NATIONALITY: | Irish | DOB: | 15.03.1983 |

DID YOU KNOW? The Republic of Ireland striker spent three separate loan spells at Ipswich Town before eventually signing permanently at Portman Road in 2013-14, and finished as the Championship's top scorer in 2014-15 with 27 goals.

Barrie McKAY | 10

| POSITION: | Midfielder | NATIONALITY: | Scottish | DOB: | 30.12.1994 |

DID YOU KNOW? McKay scored Rangers' first goal in the Third Division after their demotion before spending time away from the club on loan, but played a key part as they won promotion back to the Scottish Premiership in 2015-16.

Daniel FOX | 13

POSITION: Defender **NATIONALITY:** Scottish **DOB:** 29.05.1986

DID YOU KNOW? A cultured defender who can play at centre-back or left-back, Daniel built up a reputation as a deadly set-piece taker during his time at Coventry City and has scored plenty of goals direct from free-kicks during his career.

Ben OSBORN | 11

POSITION: Midfielder **NATIONALITY:** English **DOB:** 05.08.1994

DID YOU KNOW? Having been at the club since the age of nine, Ben has become a key figure in the first team since his debut in March 2014 and his first goal for the club came in the 92nd minute to win the game against Derby County at Pride Park in January 2015.

Matthew CASH | 14

POSITION: Midfielder **NATIONALITY:** English **DOB:** 07.08.1997

DID YOU KNOW? An energetic midfielder, Cash earned his first taste of first-team football on loan at Dagenham and Redbridge in the 2015-16 season, scoring three times in 16 appearances for the then League Two side.

Zach CLOUGH | 16

POSITION: Forward   NATIONALITY: English   DOB: 08.03.1995

DID YOU KNOW? Zach had only ever played for Bolton Wanderers prior to joining the club in January 2017, having been with the Trotters since the age of eight and going on to score 22 times in 64 appearances.

Ben BRERETON | 17

POSITION: Forward   NATIONALITY: English   DOB: 18.04.1999

DID YOU KNOW? Forward Ben broke onto the scene last season as his last-minute winner against Aston Villa at The City Ground in February gave him his first senior goal and also a vital three points for the club.

FOREST ★★

Mustapha
CARAYOL | 18

POSITION: Midfielder NATIONALITY: Gambian DOB: 04.09.1988

DID YOU KNOW? A pacy winger with a bag of tricks, Mustapha has had to work his way up to this level having played most of his early career in the lower leagues in England before getting his chance with Middlesbrough in 2012.

Kieran
DOWELL | 20

POSITION: Midfielder NATIONALITY: English DOB: 10.10.1997

DID YOU KNOW? On loan from Everton, Kieran had an excellent summer with England Under 20s as they lifted the Under 20 World Cup in South Korea, with Dowell scoring in the group stage win against the host nation.

Jamie
WARD | 19

POSITION: Midfielder NATIONALITY: Irish DOB: 12.05.1986

DID YOU KNOW? Ward is a Northern Ireland international and has featured for his country 30 times, scoring four goals. He represented the Green and White Army at Euro 2016 in France and played in all four games as they reached the Round of 16.

Jack HOBBS | 25

POSITION: Defender   NATIONALITY: English   DOB: 18.08.1988

DID YOU KNOW? Dominant centre-back Jack Hobbs signed for Nottingham Forest in 2013-14, initially on loan, from Hull City and scored his one and only goal for the club so far to win the East Midlands derby against Derby in September 2013.

David VAUGHAN | 24

POSITION: Midfielder   NATIONALITY: Welsh   DOB: 18.02.1983

DID YOU KNOW? David came through the famous Crewe Alexandra youth academy and after a brief spell in Spanish football with Real Sociedad, played his part in the exciting Blackpool team in the Premier League in the 2010-11 season.

Dimitar EVTIMOV | 26

POSITION: Goalkeeper   NATIONALITY: Bulgarian   DOB: 07.09.1993

DID YOU KNOW? The Bulgarian goalkeeper has gained experience in several loan spells after making his debut away to Leeds United in April 2014, and made his City Ground debut against Shrewsbury in the Carabao Cup in August.

Tendayi
DARIKWA | 27

POSITION: Defender **NATIONALITY:** English **DOB:** 13.12.1991

DID YOU KNOW? Tendayi was born in Nottingham and grew up in West Bridgford, he often attended games at The City Ground and returned in the summer as he joined Mark Warburton's side from Burnley for an undisclosed fee.

Stephen
HENDERSON | 30

POSITION: Goalkeeper **NATIONALITY:** Irish **DOB:** 02.05.1988

DID YOU KNOW? Stephen is the fifth goalkeeper in his family having come from a notable Irish goalkeeping family. His grandfather Paddy, dad Stephen and uncles Dave and Wayne all played professionally in Ireland and England.

Andreas
BOUCHALAKIS | 31

POSITION: Midfielder **NATIONALITY:** Greek **DOB:** 05.04.1993

DID YOU KNOW? Greek midfielder Andreas joined the club in the summer and he boasts experience of playing in European competition with Olympiacos having played in the Champions League and the Europa League.

13

FOREST
★ ★

Tyler WALKER | 34

POSITION: Forward   **NATIONALITY:** English   **DOB:** 17.10.1996

DID YOU KNOW? Striker Tyler is the son of legendary Nottingham Forest and England defender Des Walker and scored the winning goal in extra time for The Reds as they beat Newcastle United in the second round of the Carabao Cup in August.

Jason CUMMINGS | 35

POSITION: Forward   **NATIONALITY:** Scottish   **DOB:** 01.08.1995

DID YOU KNOW? Jason arrived at The City Ground in the summer with a good goalscoring record for Scottish side Hibernian, helping them to the Scottish Cup in 2015-16 and the Scottish Championship title in 2016-17.

Apostolos VELLIOS 39

POSITION: Forward   NATIONALITY: Greek   DOB: 08.01.1992

DID YOU KNOW? A Greek international who joined The Reds in June 2016, Vellios spent three years with Everton from 2011 to 2014, scoring three goals in 22 Premier League appearances during his time at Goodison Park.

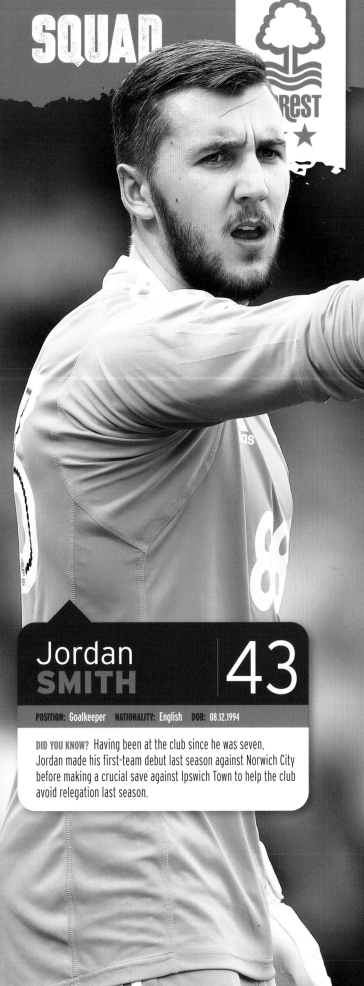

Jordan SMITH 43

POSITION: Goalkeeper   NATIONALITY: English   DOB: 08.12.1994

DID YOU KNOW? Having been at the club since he was seven, Jordan made his first-team debut last season against Norwich City before making a crucial save against Ipswich Town to help the club avoid relegation last season.

Joe WORRALL 42

POSITION: Defender   NATIONALITY: English   DOB: 10.01.1997

DID YOU KNOW? A self-confessed Forest fan, centre-back Joe came through the ranks at the club and made his first-team debut against Reading in October 2016 before captaining England to success at the Toulon Tournament last summer.

EFL SKY BET

NOTTINGHAM FOREST

CHAMPIONSHIP SQUAD

2017-18

BACK ROW: (Left to right) Chris Cohen, Michael Mancienne, Thomas Lam, Joe Worrall, Matt Mills, Danny Fox, Armand Traore, Daryl Murphy, Apostolos Vellios, Andreas Bouchalakis, Mustapha Carayol.

MIDDLE ROW: Dan Smith, Neil Simms, Tyler Walker, Ben Brereton, Jack Hobbs, Dimitar Evtimov, Jordan Smith, Stephen Henderson, Tendayi Darikwa, Eric Lichaj, Matty Cash, Nathan Beardsley, Josh Coomber, Jim Stewart.

FRONT ROW: Mick Rathbone, Andrew Balderston, Ben Osborn, Barrie McKay, Jason Cummings, David Weir, Mark Warburton, Frank McParland, Jamie Ward, Zach Clough, David Vaughan, Chris Thorpe, Will Sanders.

BARRIE 10 McKAY

SKILLS: THE CRUYFF TURN

1

2

Draw back your foot as if you are going to kick the ball

Instead of following through, stop your foot over the ball...

...and push it back behind your other leg while starting to turn your body.

3

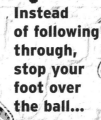

Finish turning through 180° and head in the opposite direction

4

Your unsuspecting opponent will be left standing wondering what just happened!

5

Johan Cruyff debuted his signature dummy at the 1974 FIFA World Cup. The trick is a brilliant manoeuvre to fool your opponent and change direction.

CHAMPIONSHIP KEY PLAYERS

ALEX SMITHIES
QPR

Now 27, former England U19 international Alex, was at one time rated as one of the country's hottest young goalkeepers after breaking into Huddersfield's first eleven when just 17. Despite a lot of interest, he stayed with the West Yorkshire side, playing 274 games for the Terriers until his 2015 move to the capital.

KEIREN WESTWOOD
SHEFFIELD WEDNESDAY

Keiren's excellent displays between the sticks have been rewarded with over 20 international caps for the Republic of Ireland. The excellent shot-stopper has made over 130 appearances each for Sheffield Wednesday, Coventry City and Carlisle United as well as being honoured with the Player of the Year award at each club!

ADAM DAVIES
BARNSLEY

Although Adam was born in Germany, the 25-year-old comes from a Welsh family and although he's yet to debut, he has been a part of several Wales squads. After starting his career at Everton followed by a spell with Sheffield Wednesday, Davies is now a real safe pair of hands for the Tykes with over 100 appearances behind him.

goalkeepers

The value of a great goalkeeper just can't be underestimated. We've selected six top stoppers who will look to shine over the coming months.

FELIX WIEDWALD
LEEDS UNITED

After making the move to Yorkshire from Werder Bremen in the summer, former Germany U20 international Felix really caught the eye and did so well that he was chosen ahead of Leeds United's ex-England 'keeper Rob Green. The imposing 6' 3" goalie has also played in Germany with MSV Duisburg and Eintracht Frankfurt.

VITO MANNONE
READING

Vito came to England from Atalanta and continued his career at Arsenal. Following loan spells with Barnsley and Hull City, he went north to Sunderland where he was the hero of the Black Cats' run to the 2014 League Cup final, starring in their semi-final shoot-out win against Manchester United at Old Trafford. Player of the Year at the Stadium of Light that year, Mannone moved to the Madejski Stadium last summer.

SCOTT CARSON
DERBY COUNTY

The former England goalkeeper is still one of the best 'keepers around. Scott commands his penalty area and has a real presence on the pitch. After starting out with a handful of appearances for both Leeds United and Liverpool, Carson has now played over 400 career games both in England and Turkey.

MICHAEL DAWSON
HULL CITY

Former England and Spurs centre-back, Michael made his name with Nottingham Forest before moving to the capital in 2005. The commanding defender has been voted Player of the Year with both Tottenham and the Tigers as well as winning the League Cup with Spurs a decade ago. The City skipper's consistent displays have seen him selected for the PFA Team of the Year at both ends of his career, in 2003 and 2016.

JOHN TERRY
ASTON VILLA

John is a modern-day legend. After over 700 appearances for Chelsea, and 78 for England, he had plenty of choices after leaving Stamford Bridge, but was convinced of Aston Villa's attractions by Steve Bruce, once a top-class centre-back himself. He has won everything going with Chelsea and has more individual awards than one trophy cabinet can hold.

RYAN SESSEGNON
FULHAM

Probably the best young player in the Championship, London-born Sessegnon is the cousin of the former Sunderland and WBA, Benin international Stephane Sessegnon. Ryan debuted for Fulham in August 2016 when he was only 16. Despite playing at left-back, he was joint top scorer at the 2017 European U19 tournament won with England.

defenders

Protecting a lead, battling for that all-important clean sheet and trying to help support their attack-minded teammates - here are six top quality Championship defenders to look out for.

SOULEYMANE BAMBA
CARDIFF CITY

Experienced Ivory Coast international centre-back Souleymane was born in France and began his playing career with Paris Saint-Germain before a move to Dunfermline. After plying his trade in Scotland, England, Turkey and Italy, Bamba made Wales the sixth country he has called home when he signed for Neil Warnock's Bluebirds.

NATHAN BAKER
BRISTOL CITY

After 13 years and over 100 games for Aston Villa, former England U21 international left-footed centre-back Nathan Baker signed for the Robins last summer after spending the previous season on loan at Ashton Gate. Brave and committed, Villa's loss is certainly Bristol's gain.

JOHN EGAN
BRENTFORD

The Republic of Ireland international centre-back has the happy knack of chipping in with his share of goals. He is a proper centre-back, a leader with a real hunger to keep the ball out of the net. John's dad was a famous Gaelic footballer while his mother has a League of Ireland winners medal with Cork Rangers, so it's no surprise he is a talented lad destined for the top.

CHEIKH NDOYE
BIRMINGHAM CITY

A commanding 6ft 3ins powerhouse in the centre of midfield, Senegal international Cheikh moved to St. Andrew's in 2017 from French club Angers who he skippered in last season's Coupe de France final, narrowly losing 1-0 to all conquering Paris Saint-Germain. He previously played for Creteil with whom he won the Championnat National (the third division of the French football) in 2013.

AIDEN McGEADY
SUNDERLAND

With almost 100 caps for the Republic of Ireland, Aiden is one of the most magical wingers in the Championship. In 2010 he commanded a fee of almost £10m when joining Spartak Moscow from Celtic with whom he had won seven trophies. He arrived at the Stadium of Light from Everton after playing for Black Cats boss Simon Grayson last season on loan to Preston.

DANIEL JOHNSON
PRESTON NORTH END

Originally from Kingston, Jamaica, Daniel is unmistakable with his very long hair and equally unmistakable with the energy he shows all over the pitch. He progressed through the Aston Villa academy and went on a trio of loans before Preston signed him in January 2015. Eight goals from midfield from 23 games that season helped power Preston to promotion.

midfielders

The Championship is packed with top-class midfield performers - we've chosen six midfield maestros who could well be real star turns for their respective clubs this season.

NATHAN THOMAS
SHEFFIELD UNITED

A talented and exciting winger, Nathan made the jump from, just relegated from League Two Hartlepool, to just promoted from League One Sheffield United and got off to a flying start with a debut goal in a League Cup win over Walsall. He likes to score the spectacular, finding the back of the net nine times for struggling Hartlepool last season and it's only a matter of time until Thomas is a fans' favourite at Bramall Lane.

JEM KARACAN
BOLTON WANDERERS

Jem is at his best when he's hassling and disrupting the opposition's midfield with his typically high-energy performance. London-born to an English mother and Turkish father, Jem has played for Turkey at junior levels and been in full international squads, but has yet to make his full international debut. He's played club football in Turkey as well as England and after starting over 150 games for Reading, he joined Bolton from Galatasary in 2017.

RUBEN NEVES
WOLVES

Wanderers' Portuguese international record-signing midfielder from Porto cost a reported £15.8m in 2017. Neves is just 20, but reads the game like a seasoned professional and seems destined for the top. Wolves hope this natural leader will guide them to the Premier League. Ruben is also the youngest player to captain a team in the Champions League, Porto at the age of 18.

CHAMPIONSHIP KEY PLAYERS

MARVIN SORDELL
BURTON ALBION

Still only 26, Marvin seems to have been around for a long time. He represented Great Britain at the 2012 London Olympics and has also played for England at U21 level. He made his name with Watford and once commanded a big money move into the Premier League with Bolton. He is a consistent and versatile performer who likes to shoot from distance.

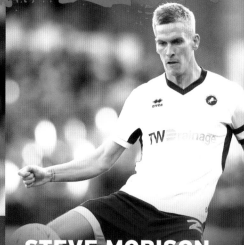

DARYL MURPHY
NOTTINGHAM FOREST

The Republic of Ireland international was the Championship's top scorer in 2014-15 with Ipswich Town when the targetman's power and pace also earned him the Tractor Boys' Player of the Year award. He won Premier League promotion with Newcastle United last season and with Sunderland in 2007 and also had a spell with Celtic in the SPL at the start of the decade.

STEVE MORISON
MILLWALL

33-year-old Steve is a Lions legend. He is now in his third spell with the club and is the reigning Millwall Player of the Year. The towering striker has scored over 230 goals in a career that started in 2001 with Northampton Town and has seen him play for England at 'C' level (non-league), before becoming a full international with Wales.

forwards

Goals win games and when it comes to finding the back of the net at Championship level, they don't come much sharper than these six great goal-getters.

BRITT ASSOMBALONGA
MIDDLESBROUGH

Britt is a proven goalscorer in the Championship, but after scoring a superb 30 goals in 47 league starts for Forest, he left the City Ground in favour of Teesside. But on his return to Nottingham with his new side in August, he must have left his shooting boots behind as missed chances meant Boro headed home empty handed. Boro invested £15m in Assombalonga and will hope he stays injury-free if they are to make a quick return to the Premier League.

NELSON OLIVEIRA
NORWICH CITY

The Portugal international is a threatening striker, quick off the mark with first-class technique and neat footwork. Nelson, who started with Benfica, had six loans with clubs in Portugal, France, England and Wales, before committing his future to the Carrow Road club in 2016. He scored 15 times in 31 games in his first season as a Canary and commenced the current campaign with three goals in his first three matches.

MARTYN WAGHORN
IPSWICH TOWN

The former England U21 international returned to the English league last summer after two years in Scotland with Rangers where he won a Player of the Year award to go with the Young Player of the Year trophy he won with Leicester. Martyn has the ability to play anywhere across the front four and his good scoring record continued this season with four goals in his first three Championship games.

MATT 5
MILLS

A real fans' favourite at the City Ground, Stuart Pearce played a staggering 524 games for Forest and hammered home an incredible 89 goals from the left-back berth, during an unforgettable 12-year spell with the club.

Pearce was recruited from Coventry City by legendry Forest boss Brian Clough in 1985 and went on to taste domestic success at club level while also making the England left-back shirt his own.

A robust and fully-committed defender, Pearce's determination saw him idolised by the City Ground faithful who almost viewed him as a supporter on the pitch, such was his commitment to the club. An inspirational leader, Pearce spent the majority of his City Ground career as captain.

Part of an excellent Forest team in the late 80s and early 90s, Pearce and his teammates reached a hat-trick of consecutive League Cup finals at Wembley. Forest were League Cup winners in 1989 after defeating Luton Town 3-1. They regained the trophy the following season with a narrow 1-0 success over Oldham Athletic, but suffered defeat to Manchester United, 1-0, in 1991.

Pearce also made three other trips to Wembley with the club and was twice a Full Members Cup winner as Forest defeated Everton in 1989 and Southampton in 1992.

However, his most memorable club appearance at Wembley was during the 1991 FA Cup final, when he opened the scoring with yet another of his trademark thunderbolt free-kicks.

Sadly, opponents Spurs recovered from both the loss of Paul Gascoigne, and falling a goal behind, to win the match 2-1.

Despite Forest's relegation from the Premier League in 1993 and Clough's retirement, Pearce stayed at the City Ground and helped new manager Frank Clark steer the Club back to the top flight at the first attempt. He was then part of the team that finished third in the Premier League in 1994-95 and reached the UEFA Cup quarter-finals a year later.

Pearce ended his Forest playing career in 1997 and returned to the City Ground as manager in July 2014. Although his time in charge was not the success everyone at the City Ground had hoped for, he remains a true Nottingham Forest giant.

STUART PEARCE

TRAINING TO WIN

Footballers are finely-tuned athletes with impressive skills which they need to demonstrate under pressure. They have to be physically and mentally strong.

The world's top sports-stars face tough challenges in their chosen field, but they can be very different to those that a footballer has to face. In sports such as golf, athletics and even tennis or a team game like cricket, you have no-one physically trying to stop you when you're attempting to play the game.

However, think about what you have to do as a footballer. You have to have the ability to control the ball, even when it comes to you at speed or a difficult angle. You have to be able to pass over short and long distances. You have to be able to head the ball. Not every player can do it all, but at least some members of the team have to be able to shoot well and tackle too.

All this would be hard enough without having your opponent doing his utmost to stop you - holding you, pushing you, knocking you off balance and quite possibly fouling you. So a footballer has to have strength and speed as well as skill.

To become a professional footballer, firstly, you have to have bundles of skill which you've probably spent all your life developing, but you also have to be extremely fit. Footballers do all kinds of exercise to get fit, and stay fit. They work in the gym to build up their strength and they also work with fitness coaches who keep them in peak physical condition.

They have to be very careful to follow a healthy diet. If they don't, it makes it hard for them to stay match fit. They avoid foods with lots of fat, so they rarely eat things like crisps, chocolate, chips and burgers, if at all.

Once they have reached full fitness for the start of the season, footballers usually train for about two hours a day, four or five days a week if they have one game a week. It is important that they also rest at the right times or they won't feel at their best during games. Some players will also do other exercises like pilates or yoga to help them stay supple.

There is a lot to being a professional footballer. Staying in peak condition requires a lot of dedication and players who look after themselves well by eating healthily and training hard will be able to give their team and fans 100% on the pitch.

GOAL OF THE SEASON

FOREST ★ ★

Apostolos Vellios

V ROTHERHAM · 14 SEPTEMBER 2016

Apostolos Vellios' stunning overhead-kick against Rotherham was voted the 2016-17 Goal of the Season by the Forest fans. The Greek forward's acrobatic attempt put Forest 2-1 up late on in the match, before the game eventually finished 2-2 at the New York Stadium.

Jon Taylor put the Millers into a first-half lead with a side-footed finish, before Forest hit back in the second half. Matt Mills' header from a corner found its way into the net on 76 minutes before the home side were reduced to ten men after Darnell Fisher's red card for two bookable offences.

With five minutes to go, Vellios struck with his Goal of the Season to send the packed away end into hysteria. Mills nodded a free-kick back across goal and the ball sat up nicely for Vellios to fling himself acrobatically into the air to hit the ball into the roof of the net from eight yards out, giving goalkeeper and former Forest player Lee Camp no chance.

The scoring wasn't done there though as the ten men of Rotherham equalised two minutes later as Taylor grabbed his second of the game to seal a point.

In an end of season poll, Nottingham Forest supporters voted in their thousands to choose their Goal of the Season.

Vellios' strike was one of eight shortlisted and he won the majority of the fans' votes, beating Ben Osborn's free-kick against Bristol City and Hildeberto Pereira's solo effort against Birmingham City to the crown.

DARYL 9
MURPHY

29

FOREST
★ ★

There have been many great double acts at the City Ground over the years...

Solid defensive partnerships, creative midfield pairings and prolific goalscoring duos.

But unquestionably, the finest double act in the club's history was that of manager Brian Clough and his assistant Peter Taylor who combined to bring the club its greatest triumphs.

The fortunes of Nottingham Forest Football Club, its players, staff and supporters, all changed in 1975 when Brian Clough became manager at the City Ground. The transformation of the club was truly remarkable and all made possible by the unique chemistry that existed between Clough and his assistant Taylor.

DOUBLE
CLOUGH

Clough checked in at the City Ground ahead of Taylor who joined him in 1976, reuniting the partnership they had enjoyed at Hartlepool, Derby County and Brighton. When Taylor and Clough took over at Forest, the club was in the Second Division (today's Championship) but within a season they were back in the top flight.

Promotion from the Second Division was gained in 1976-77 as the club sealed the third and final promotion berth behind Chelsea and champions Wolverhampton Wanderers.

A truly unforgettable season followed in 1977-78 as Forest took the First Division by storm, first winning the League Cup and then against all odds confirming themselves as First Division champions. The League Cup triumph was achieved following a replay.

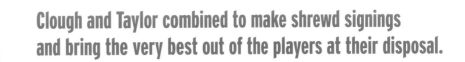
Clough and Taylor combined to make shrewd signings and bring the very best out of the players at their disposal.

After overseeing the league title triumph in 1977-78, the duo went on to lead the club on to even greater success in Europe.

Clough and Taylor created their legendary status by securing two European Cup wins, firstly in 1979 and then remarkably regaining the trophy in 1980. The team defeated Swedish side Malmo in the first final in 1979 thanks to a Trevor Francis goal.

German club Hamburg were beaten by a single strike from the mercurial John Robertson a year later as Forest became back-to-back European champions.

ACTS & TAYLOR

Forest had drawn 0-0 with favourites Liverpool at Wembley before a John Robertson penalty sealed victory in the replay at Old Trafford. Just a month after their League Cup success, they were crowned First Division champions - ending the season with a seven-point cushion over runners-up Liverpool.

It was a truly remarkable achievement for a club such as Nottingham Forest and why the Clough/Taylor partnership is so fondly remembered.

BEN **11**
OSBORN

FOOTBALL 50

Here is a list of 50 footie words. All but one are hidden in the grid, can you work out which is missing?

FOREST ★★

```
S U B S T I T U T E I S R E D L E I F D I M
M A A Z P L E A O S U J Y O Y T N D T R K O
A Q E X T R A T I M E R L C K J A U D I M E
N B L C A C A D E M Y K F Y U K O B C B N P
O N I E S A J W R T P E X R T G D K H B P B
F R F J A P H I A E M R Y C U C O C A L T L
T H I W Y T D B K W S T O D Y F B R L I E I
H D N E P A R X J B I S C M F A U O L N E T
E D A Z L I N E S M A N I T O F D G E G H R
M B L D S N W A E C Q I U N A T P U N Q S A
A I W Y H C O R N E R F L A G O I M G Z N N
T E H E A D E R V L H Y S R I R C O E R A S
C B I M J E E L U R E D I S F F O K N V E F
H G S G Q F P R N U A L K L G I H O B M L E
F R T U F E L N B T F E R E G A N A M A C R
M E L K E N G F B Y D H T D A F V G O H J W
Y K E F C D R P O C M F H L H J W G A B H I
S I O W O E K S P U I A O A V S N F D M I N
A R W M N R Q N R P L H T U O E M S R T J D
O T K C I K E E R F Y T D C D J Y B A G T O
G S O V T C A D T B R X N L H S F A C U P W
K A M P Q E T I C I E F O M R N G E W B S U
C I A M S K M R C A S G C G O U K O O C E M
I Y E J A E R K D I R F H S R E Y A L P V C
K C T E P D R G B F K D A E U G A E L E R S
R E T L T N W T J N G E Q U A L I S E R E H
O Y S P A I A W N G S R C V S F G L Y F S R
S S R N T N H L H E L S U N U T M E G U E N
S K I J S J E V R L C W A S P O L S O F R J
I K F P F H M P L K U F E H E L A O E T I M
C R O S S B A R S C T T M R O J I R W T Q N
S O I R M E X I C A N W A V E P E O L D K P
G A S U N N A E R T U B R E P E E K L A O G
```

Word List:

ACADEMY
CAPTAIN
CENTRE SPOT
CHALLENGE
CLEAN SHEET
CORNER FLAG
CROSSBAR
DEFENDER
DERBY MATCH
DRESSING ROOM
DRIBBLING
DUGOUT
EQUALISER
EXTRA TIME
FA CUP
FANS
FINAL WHISTLE
FIRST TEAM
FIXTURE
FOUL
FREE KICK
GOALKEEPER
GOLDEN GOAL
HALF TIME
HAT-TRICK
HEADER
INJURY TIME
KICK-OFF
LEAGUE
LINESMAN
MANAGER
MAN OF THE MATCH
MEXICAN WAVE
MIDFIELDER
NUTMEG
OFFSIDE RULE
PENALTY
PLAYERS
PRE-SEASON
PROMOTION
RED CARD
REFEREE
RESERVES
SCISSOR KICK
STRIKER
SUBSTITUTE
TACKLE
TRANSFER WINDOW
VOLLEY
YELLOW CARD

ANSWERS ON PAGE 62

2017 PLAYER OF THE YEAR

As one of Nottingham Forest's most consistent performers in the 2016-17 season, Eric Lichaj was crowned as the club's Player of the Year.

The club's supporters were put to the vote to have their say on who should lift the trophy after the final game of the season, and the American defender's work-rate and consistent displays were enough for him to win the award.

Just over 1,000 Forest supporters had their say on who was the stand-out performer and Lichaj secured more than 40 per cent of the vote, with Ben Osborn in second place and David Vaughan in third.

After picking up his award, Lichaj said: "I am really happy, not at the state of the season as a whole, but at avoiding relegation and it is an honour that I will remember for the rest of my life.

"It does make it extra special knowing that the fans have voted for me; it is a good award to have. I know that Dorus De Vries won it last year and that was well deserved for him. I don't know if I deserved it this year as it has been a difficult season, but I do really appreciate it."

Lichaj featured 45 times in all competitions for The Reds in 2016-17, scoring twice in the wins against Birmingham City and Huddersfield Town at The City Ground and he went on to play a key role for his country at the Gold Cup in the summer. The full-back scored in the win against El Salvador before helping the US to win the tournament altogether.

PLAYERS OF THE SEASON
FROM TONY WOODCOCK TO ERIC LICHAJ

1977

1979

1983

1977	Tony Woodcock
1978	Kenny Burns
1979	Garry Birtles
1980	Larry Lloyd
1981	Kenny Burns
1982	Peter Shilton
1983	Steve Hodge
1984	Chris Fairclough
1985	Jim McInally
1986	Nigel Clough
1987	Des Walker
1988	Nigel Clough
1989	Stuart Pearce
1990	Des Walker
1991	Stuart Pearce
1992	Des Walker
1993	Steve Sutton
1994	Dave Philips
1995	Steve Stone
1996	Stuart Pearce
1997	Colin Cooper
1998	Pierre van Hooijdonk
1999	Alan Rogers
2000	Dave Beasant
2001	Chris Bart-Williams
2002	Gareth Williams
2003	David Johnson
2004	Andy Reid
2005	Paul Gerrard
2006	Ian Breckin
2007	Grant Holt
2008	Julian Bennett
2009	Chris Cohen
2010	Lee Camp
2011	Luke Chambers
2012	Garath McCleary
2013	Chris Cohen
2014	Andy Reid
2015	Michail Antonio
2016	Dorus de Vries
2017	Eric Lichaj

1986 & 88

2000

1987, 90 & 92

2004 & 14

1995

2007

2010

SKILLS: THE RAINBOW KICK

1 Start off with your feet on either side of the ball

2 Use one foot to roll the ball up your other leg

3 Make sure to roll the ball hard enough to give it some air

4 When the ball is in the air strike it with your heel

5 ...and flick it over your head!

Brazilian star striker, Neymar, is well known for his use of the rainbow kick on the pitch and regularly fools his opposition. The trick is an impressive show of skill which takes practise, practise practise!

TIP: Lean forward as you're doing the trick, this helps create space between you and the ball so you can strike it more easily.

MICHAEL
MANCIENNE

FOREST
★★

ASTON VILLA

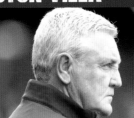

Which England and Chelsea legend did Aston Villa sign at the start of this season?

1 ANSWER

Aston Villa won the European Cup in 1981. Did they beat Bayern Munich, Barcelona or Real Madrid in the final?

2 ANSWER

Who is the former Sunderland manager who started the season as Villa manager?

3 ANSWER

BARNSLEY

During the summer Barnsley signed Ezekiel Fryers from which Premier League London club?

5 ANSWER

Who is Barnsley's captain?

4 ANSWER

Who is the Tykes' manager?

6 ANSWER

BIRMINGHAM CITY

When did Blues last win the League Cup?

8 ANSWER

Who scored Blues first league goal this season?

7 ANSWER

City completed a record signing on transfer deadline day, summer 2017. Who was it?

9 ANSWER

BOLTON WANDERERS

How many times have Bolton won the FA Cup?

10 ANSWER

Bolton reached the League Cup final in 2004, but lost to which club who are also now in the Championship?

11 ANSWER

Name the manager who led Bolton to promotion in 2017 in his first season at the club.

12 ANSWER

BRENTFORD

Brentford are West London rivals of QPR who they knocked out of this season's Carabao Cup away from home. Did they win 3-1, 4-1 or 5-1?

13 ANSWER

Who is Brentford's Number 9 striker this season?

14 ANSWER

Who was the manager of Brentford from 2013 to 2015 who went on to manage Rangers and Nottingham Forest?

15 ANSWER

BRISTOL CITY

Which Premier League team did City knock out of the Carabao Cup away from home in the second round this season?

17 ANSWER

Who was Bristol City's Player of the Season in 2016-17?

16 ANSWER

Who scored 23 times for Bristol City last season on loan from Chelsea?

18 ANSWER

CHALLENGE

Let's see how well you know Forest and their Championship rivals...

FOREST ★★

BURTON ALBION

Who was Burton's first summer signing ahead of the 2017-18 season?

20 ANSWER

Which former England international began the season as Burton's manager?

19 ANSWER

Which former Liverpool and Villa player signed for Burton at the start of the season?

21 ANSWER

CARDIFF CITY

Cardiff City are the Bluebirds, but what colour were their shirts between 2012 and 2015?

22 ANSWER

Who was the Chile international midfielder who moved from Cardiff to Inter Milan in 2014 and stayed with the Italian giants until 2017?

24 ANSWER

Who was the manager that inspired Cardiff to maximum points from their first five league games of this season?

23 ANSWER

DERBY COUNTY

Which Derby player scored the opening goal at the Stadium of Light this season?

25 ANSWER

In what year did Derby win the FA Cup?

26 ANSWER

Who is the former England international Derby re-signed for a second spell at the club at the start of this season?

27 ANSWER

FULHAM

Who is Fulham's No 1 this season?

29 ANSWER

Which Spanish side beat Fulham in the final of the 2010 Europa League?

28 ANSWER

Who is Fulham's No 10 and their captain this season?

30 ANSWER

HULL CITY

Which country did Leonid Slutsky manage before taking over at Hull?

32 ANSWER

What is Hull's nickname?

31 ANSWER

Hull reached the FA Cup final in 2014 but lost to which London club?

33 ANSWER

IPSWICH TOWN

Who scored Town's first league goal this season?

34 ANSWER

Ipswich went from the third division to top-flight champions in six years under the manager who later won the World Cup for England. Who was that?

35 ANSWER

In which season did the Tractor Boys win the FA Cup?

36 ANSWER

LEEDS UNITED

What is Leeds United's club anthem?

37 ANSWER

Between 1965 and 1974 how many times did Leeds finish in the top two of the league?

38 ANSWER

Who is captaining the Whites this season?

39

MIDDLESBROUGH

Which Spanish team beat Middlesbrough in the 2006 Europa League final?

41 ANSWER

Who did Boro sign on a season-long loan from Swansea City in July 2017?

40 ANSWER

Which major trophy did Boro win in 2004?

42

MILLWALL

Who did Millwall play in the 2004 FA Cup final?

44 ANSWER

Millwall began this season with one of their former Players of the Year as manager. Who?

43 ANSWER

What is Millwall's nickname?

45 ANSWER

NORWICH CITY

Which team did Head Coach, Daniel Farke, manage before joining City this season?

46 ANSWER

How many League Cup finals have Norwich played in, two, three or four?

47

Who is the Canaries No 1 this season?

48

NOTTINGHAM FOREST

Which Premier League club did Forest defeat away from home in the Carabao Cup in August 2017?

49 ANSWER

Forest have twice won the European Cup (now the Champions League). True or false?

50 ANSWER

Who is the former Brighton, Leeds and Sunderland midfielder Forest signed in August 2017?

51 ANSWER

PRESTON NORTH END

Who was the future Everton and Manchester United manager who won the Division Two title with Preston in 2000?

53 ANSWER

Who was Preston's top scorer last season?

52 ANSWER

Preston did it first in 1996, Wolves equalled it in 1988 and Burnley, Sheffield United and Portsmouth have done it since. What is the feat these five clubs have achieved?

54 ANSWER

CHALLENGE

Let's see how well you know Forest and their Championship rivals...

FOREST ★★

QUEENS PARK RANGERS

Who is QPR's captain this season?

55

Which defender did Rangers pay a club record £12.5m for in 2013 only to sell him later that year?

56

Which of the following managers have not managed QPR: Harry Redknapp, Mark Hughes, Martin O'Neill and Ian Holloway?

57

READING

Which former Manchester United defender was manager of Reading at the start of the season?

58

What position in the Championship did Reading finish in last season?

59

Who did Reading sign from Sunderland during the summer?

60

SHEFFIELD UNITED

Who is the Blades' No 9 striker this season?

61

How many points did Sheffield United earn in winning League One last season: 95, 100 or 105?

62

Goalkeeper Jamal Blackman is on a season-long loan to Sheffield United from which Premier League London club?

63

SHEFFIELD WEDNESDAY

Who was Sheffield Wednesday's first 2017 summer signing?

64

Sheffield Wednesday are one of the oldest clubs in the world. In 2017 they celebrated a major anniversary. How many years old were the club in 2017?

65

Adding together Sheffield Wednesday's top flight league titles, FA Cup and League Cup wins, how many major trophies have they won: 6, 7 or 8?

66

SUNDERLAND

Who did Sunderland sign from West Brom on August 2017 transfer deadline day?

67

How many other current Championship clubs have Sunderland met in FA Cup finals?

68

Which two academy produced players scored their first goals for the club in August 2017?

69

WOLVERHAMPTON WANDERERS

Who were last season's League Cup finalists that Wolves knocked out of this season's Carabao Cup in August?

70

Between 1950 and 1960 how many times did Wolves finish in the top two of the top flight?

71

Who is the Portuguese midfielder Wolves paid almost £16m in the summer of 2017?

72

ARMAND TRAORE 6

SKILLS: THE MARADONA SPIN

1 Start off by simply dribbling the ball

2 While moving in a forward motion, tap the ball with your leading foot...

3 ...and start turning your body in the opposite direction

4

5 As you're spinning, pull the ball back with your other foot while continuing to turn

6 Then keep moving forward!

Argentinian maestro, Maradona, is very well known for this move. It is brilliant for overcoming opponents and getting yourself into space, as while you are spinning you are putting your back to the defender and shielding the ball.

WHATBALL?

There are too many footballs!

Work out which is the real ball in each photo.

WALLY ARDRON

Prolific goalscorer Wally Ardron holds the record for scoring the most goals in a single season for Nottingham Forest - the ace marksman netted a phenomenal 36 goals in 1950-51 as Forest were crowned Division Three South champions.

Ardron's proud record has stood for over half a century and is unlikely to ever be surpassed. Remarkably, Forest is not the only club that Ardron also holds the title for the number of goals scored in a season. He netted 38 goals in 1946-47 for Rotherham United in the Millers' Division Three (North) campaign. Suffice to say Forest and Rotherham fans are still to this day craving a goalscorer of his ilk!

So prolific was Ardron in front goal that be became the first post-war player to score 200 league goals.

Ardron was born in Swinton, South Yorkshire on 19 September 1918 and began his playing career at Millmoor with Rotherham United. A remarkable aspect of his career is that Ardron's first game in the Football League was on 14 January 1939 and his second was on 31 August 1946.

Of course, the Second World War intervened, but nevertheless, seven years and 228 days is an unprecedented interval between a player's first two senior games, particularly when he went on to play a further 304 Football League games.

He joined Forest in June 1949 after Rotherham United accepted a then club record fee received of £10,000 for his services. Aged 32 when he arrived at the City Ground, Ardron looked upon the move as a new career and wasted little time in winning the respect and admiration of the Forest supporters with both his performances and goals.

A true Forest legend, Ardron had a serious appetite for goals as his record of 123 league goals in 183 league matches for Nottingham Forest goes to prove.

FOREST ★★

The prolific strike-partnership of Kevin Campbell and Pierre van Hooijdonk combined to score a memorable 52 league goals during the 1997-98 campaign as Forest secured an immediate return to the Premier League as First Division Champions.

DOUBLE

Having suffered relegation from the Premier League the previous season along with Sunderland and Middlesbrough, Forest stormed to the First Division title under the management of Dave Bassett and secured the top slot with an impressive 94-point haul.

Promotion was achieved via a great team effort, but the season is particularly remembered for the goals of Campbell and van Hooijdonk, who often just proved too hot to handle for opposing defences.

Campbell was the first to arrive at the City Ground. After beginning his career with Arsenal, he fell down the pecking order at Highbury due to the form and goals of Ian Wright and Dennis Bergkamp. He joined Forest in the summer of 1995 for an initial fee believed to have been in the region of £2.5m. Ironically, Campbell's first goal for Forest came against his former employers in a 1-1 draw at Highbury in August 1995

He scored three goals in 21 games in his first season at Forest as the team finished the campaign in a creditable ninth place in the Premier League. Campbell was part of the 1996-97 squad that ended the following season propping up the Premier League, but stayed to produce his most prolific campaign with the club and ensure promotion the following season.

CAMPBELL &

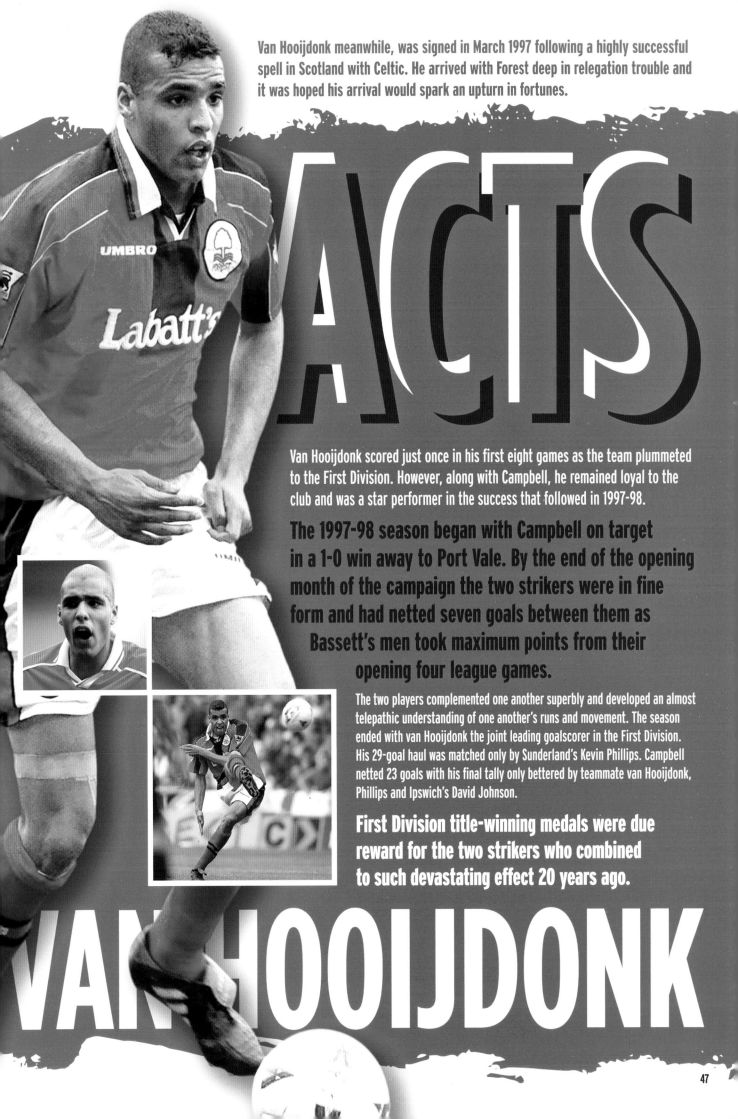

Van Hooijdonk meanwhile, was signed in March 1997 following a highly successful spell in Scotland with Celtic. He arrived with Forest deep in relegation trouble and it was hoped his arrival would spark an upturn in fortunes.

ACTS

Van Hooijdonk scored just once in his first eight games as the team plummeted to the First Division. However, along with Campbell, he remained loyal to the club and was a star performer in the success that followed in 1997-98.

The 1997-98 season began with Campbell on target in a 1-0 win away to Port Vale. By the end of the opening month of the campaign the two strikers were in fine form and had netted seven goals between them as Bassett's men took maximum points from their opening four league games.

The two players complemented one another superbly and developed an almost telepathic understanding of one another's runs and movement. The season ended with van Hooijdonk the joint leading goalscorer in the First Division. His 29-goal haul was matched only by Sunderland's Kevin Phillips. Campbell netted 23 goals with his final tally only bettered by teammate van Hooijdonk, Phillips and Ipswich's David Johnson.

First Division title-winning medals were due reward for the two strikers who combined to such devastating effect 20 years ago.

VAN HOOIJDONK

Design their kit,
add hair, be creative!

MAKE YOUR OWN
FOOZBALL
TEAM

FOREST
★ ★

ZACH **16**
CLOUGH

FOREST ★★

WORLD CUP

WHEN THE SEASON COMES TO AN END IN THE SUMMER, THE FOOTBALL DOESN'T STOP THERE!...

When Forest's campaign is over and the Championship prizes are handed out, you can sit back and get ready to watch the World's international superstars take to the pitch for the 2018 FIFA World Cup which starts on 14 June.

Just to get you in the mood, try this World Cup quiz!

1930

The first World Cup was won by the host nation Uruguay, but who did they defeat 4-2 in the Final?

1950

During England's first-ever World Cup in Brazil, they were beaten 1-0 by a team of part-timers from which Country?

1966

Forest's mascot is Sherwood the Bear, but what was the official World Cup mascot called when England beat Germany 4-2 to win the World Cup?

1934

The host nation were victorious again! Italy beat Czechoslovakia 2-1, but do you know how many times the Italians have won the World Cup?

1954

Which country scored 27 goals, the most of the tournament? Ferenc Puskás netted four!

1970

Arguably the greatest World Cup final of all time was in 1970, when brilliant Brazil won 4-1. Who did they beat?

1938

Italy retained the trophy with a 4-2 victory over Hungary, in which European capital?

1958 & 1962

The same name went on the trophy in 1958 and 1962, the first and second of their record five wins. Who are they?

1974

The Dutch captain produced one of the World Cup's most iconic moments - a 180 degree wrong-footing turn that totally outwitted the defender. What is the move called?

QUIZ....

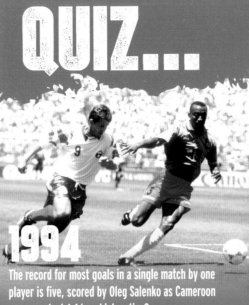

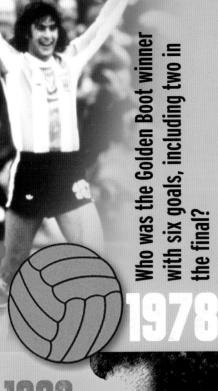

1978

Who was the Golden Boot winner with six goals, including two in the final?

1994

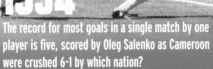

The record for most goals in a single match by one player is five, scored by Oleg Salenko as Cameroon were crushed 6-1 by which nation?

2006

One match, nicknamed 'the Battle of Nuremberg' ended nine-a-side as 16 yellow cards and four red cards were handed out. Who were the teams and what was the result?

1982

England were unbeaten in five games and only conceded one goal in the tournament. Which former Forest 'keeper was between the sticks?

1998

Who won the Golden Ball award for the tournament's best player?

2010

Only one country remained unbeaten throughout the whole tournament. Which nation was it?

1986

Which legendary Argentinian scored twice to knock England out at the quarter-final stage 2-1?

2002

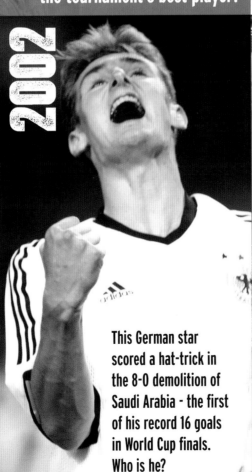

This German star scored a hat-trick in the 8-0 demolition of Saudi Arabia - the first of his record 16 goals in World Cup finals. Who is he?

2014

Which country staged the last World Cup in 2014 and who are the World Cup holders?

1990

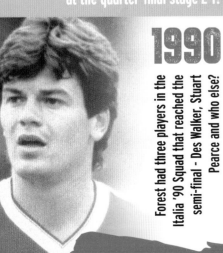

Forest had three players in the Italia '90 Squad that reached the semi-final - Des Walker, Stuart Pearce and who else?

2018

Where are the World Cup finals going to be held next summer?

Garry Monk ☐   Neil Warnock ☐   Jaap Stam ☐   Steve Bruce ☐   Mick McCarthy ☐

Can you find them all?

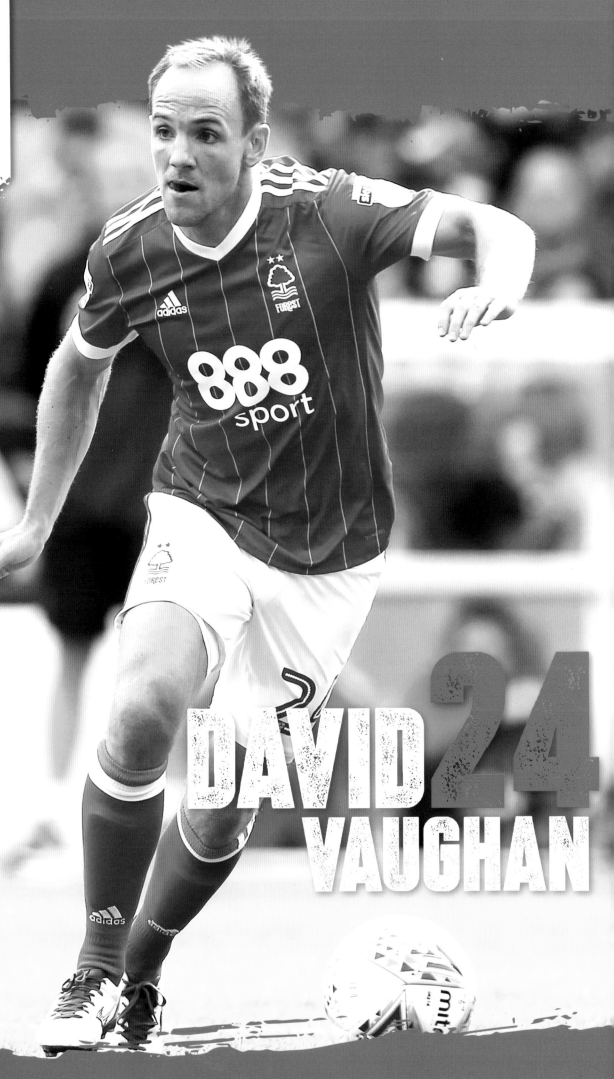

DAVID 24
VAUGHAN

CULT heroes

Widely regarded as the finest Nottingham Forest player of all time, Scottish international midfielder John Robertson was a star performer in Brian Clough's formidable side that were twice crowned European champions.

Robertson had played for Scotland as a schoolboy before joining Forest in May 1970. His debut came in the October under the management of Matt Gillies, but he was an infrequent member of the first team and was remarkably on the transfer list when Clough became manager in January 1975.

Clough instantly spotted Robertson's outstanding ability to run with the ball and cross with the most incredible accuracy. From the moment Clough walked into the City Ground, Robertson's career took off.

The skilful left-winger was one of the first names on Clough's teamsheet and played an incredible 243 consecutive games in a four-year spell between December 1976 and December 1980.

After helping Forest win promotion from the Second Division in 1976-77, Robertson netted the winning goal from the penalty spot in the 1978 League Cup final replay as Forest lifted the trophy thanks to a 1-0 victory over Liverpool at Old Trafford.

The League Cup win spurred Robertson and his teammates on to even greater achievements in 1977-78 as against all odds, they lifted the First Division title in their first season back in the top flight. Robertson ended the campaign as the side's ever-present top scorer with 12 league goals and a host of assists for centre-forwards Peter Withe and Tony Woodcock.

After becoming a First Division champion in 1977-78, Robertson starred in both of Forest's European Cup triumphs of 1979 and 1980. He provided the cross for Trevor Francis' winning goal in the 1-0 win over Malmo in 1979 and then proceeded to be the hero of the hour himself when he scored the only goal of the game in the 1980 final against Hamburg.

Robertson played over 500 games for Forest, but his contribution in making them kings of Europe will always see him revered at the City Ground.

JOHN ROBERTSON

FOREST

You would definitely recognise the City Ground, but can you figure out which football club these grounds are home to...

1

Team: _____
Ground: _____
Capacity: _____

2

Team: _____
Ground: _____
Capacity: _____

3

Team: _____
Ground: _____
Capacity: _____

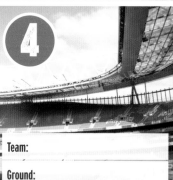

4

Team: _____
Ground: _____
Capacity: _____

5

Team: _____
Ground: _____
Capacity: _____

6

Team: _____
Ground: _____
Capacity: _____

7

8

Team: _____
Ground: _____
Capacity: _____

Team: _____
Ground: _____
Capacity: _____

9

10

Team: _____
Ground: _____
Capacity: _____

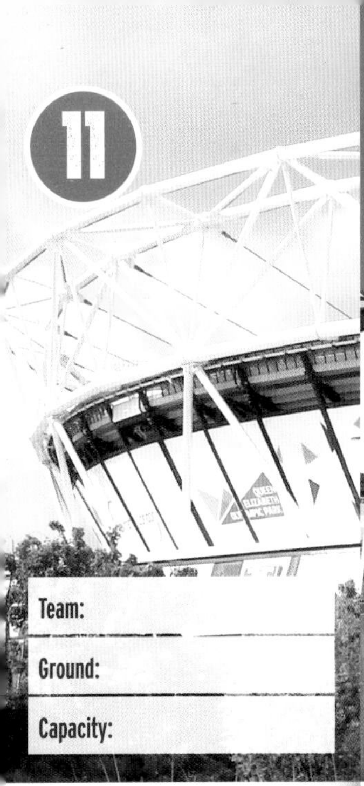

11

Team:

Ground:

Capacity:

...as well as their official name and capacity?!

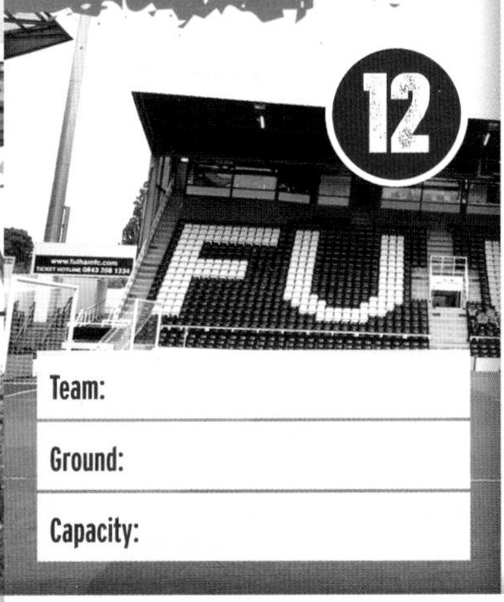

12

Team:

Ground:

Capacity:

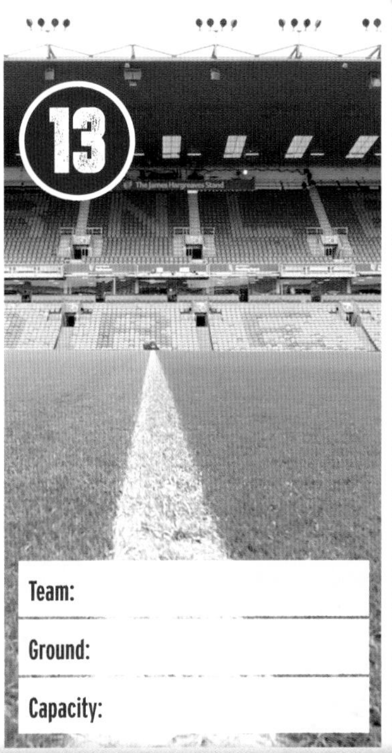

13

Team:

Ground:

Capacity:

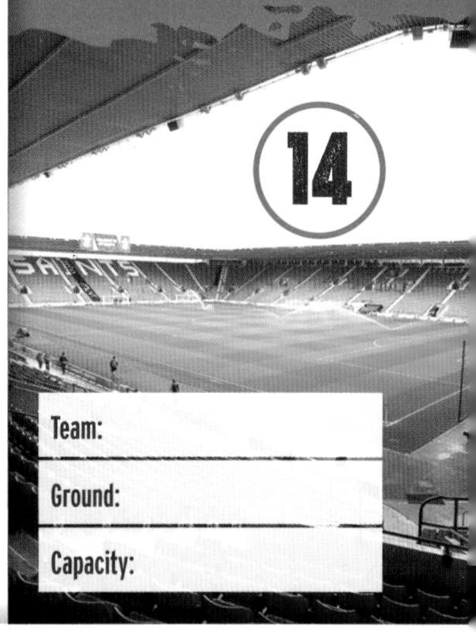

14

Team:

Ground:

Capacity:

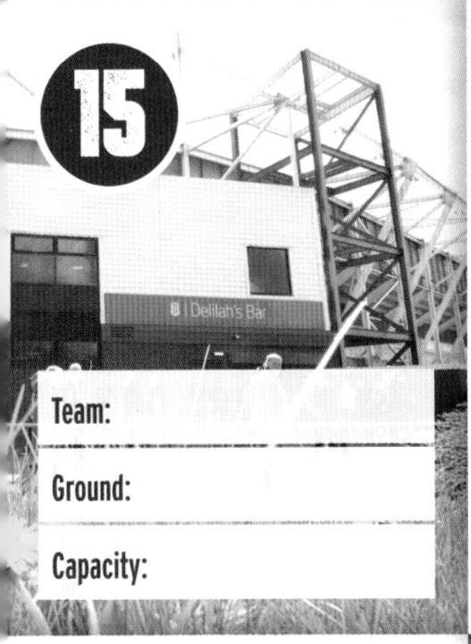

15

Team:

Ground:

Capacity:

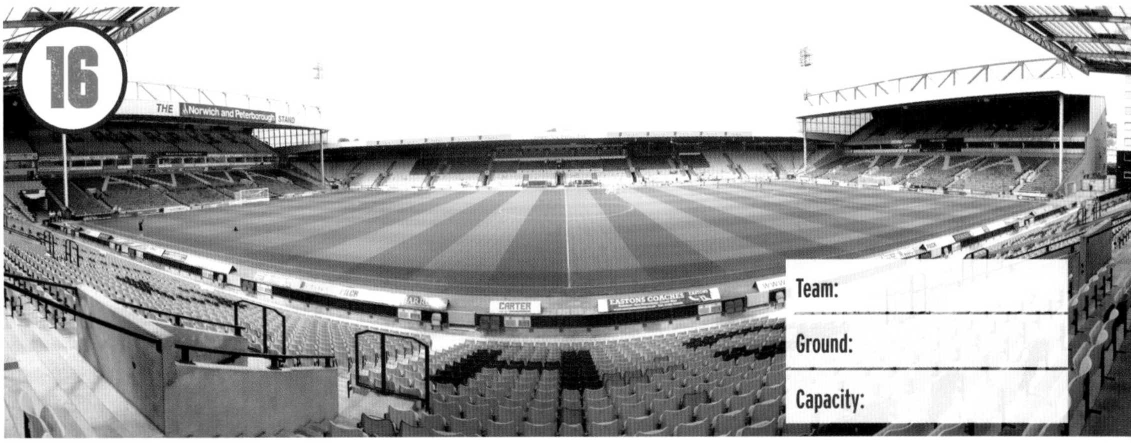

16

Team:

Ground:

Capacity:

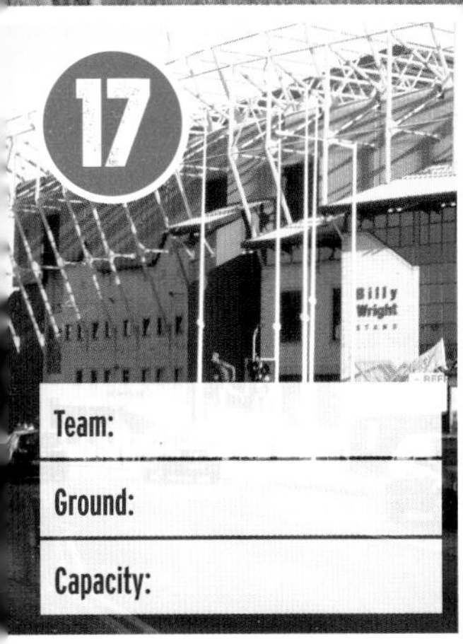

17

Team:

Ground:

Capacity:

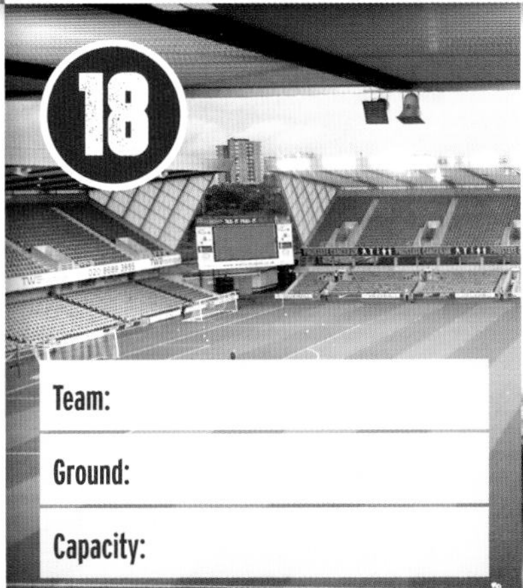

18

Team:

Ground:

Capacity:

19

Team:

Ground:

Capacity:

20

Team:

Ground:

Capacity:

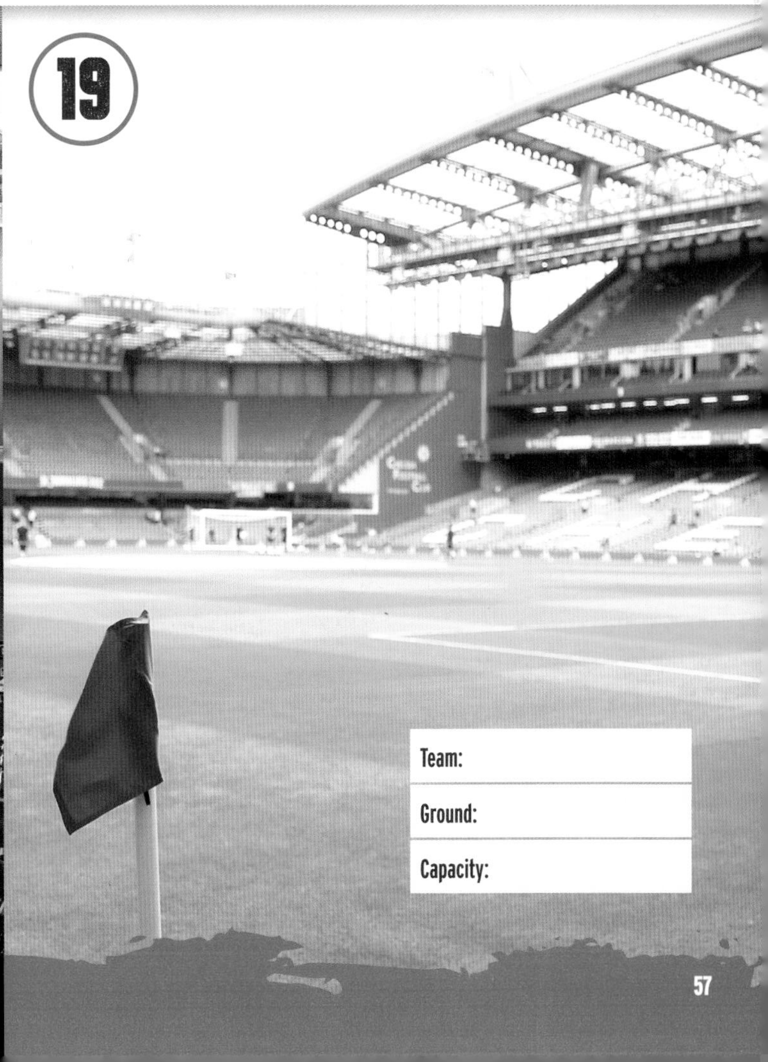

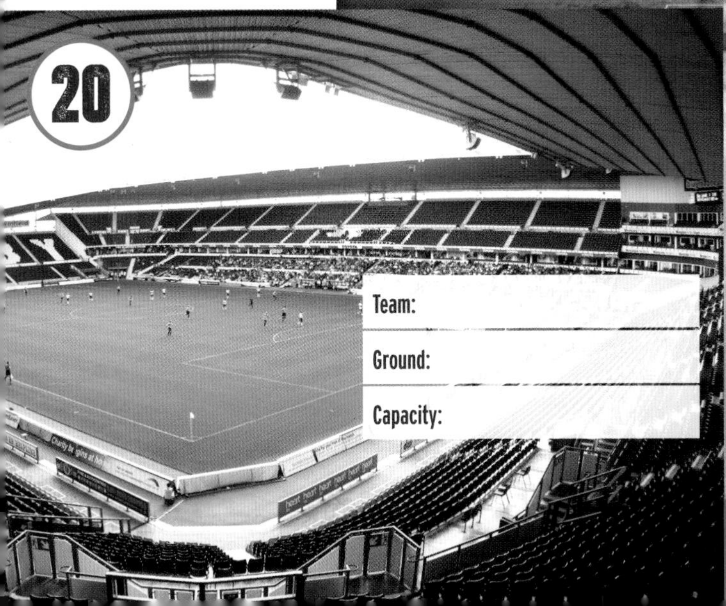

FIVE GAMES TO LOOK OUT FOR IN...

DERBY COUNTY (H) – SATURDAY 10 MARCH

The second East Midlands derby of the season takes place in March and is always one of the most eagerly-anticipated fixtures of the season. Last season saw Forest score a dramatic injury-time equaliser against their arch rivals thanks to a Dani Pinillos header and more drama is expected on Trentside for the clash against Gary Rowett's side.

LEEDS UNITED (A) · MONDAY 1 JANUARY

Forest begin 2018 with a trip to Elland Road to take on Leeds United. The Whites made a strong start to the season, including picking up three points at The City Ground, and Mark Warburton's men will be looking to take all three points to kickstart the New Year and compete with a side expected to be competing near the top end of the table.

BARNSLEY (H) – MONDAY 2 APRIL

The Easter weekend is normally one of the defining weekends in the season and Forest entertain Barnsley at The City Ground on Easter Monday. Fresh off the back of the trip to Millwall on Good Friday, Mark Warburton's men will entertain Paul Heckingbottom's side in the hope that they are right in the mix near the top of the table.

WOLVES (A) – SATURDAY 27 JANUARY

Another team expected to be challenging are Wolves who spent big in the summer to bring in young talent from the continent. Nuno Espirito Santo's side have been playing some attractive football and getting results so Mark Warburton's side will be keen to show what they can do when they make the trip to Molineux.

BOLTON WANDERERS (A) – SUNDAY 6 MAY

The Reds end the 2017-18 season away to Bolton Wanderers and will hope to have something to play for at the Macron Stadium in May. Last season's last day saw Forest needing a win to survive in the Championship, but The Reds will be hoping to be in with a shout of a top six finish come the final day of this campaign.

THE SECOND HALF OF THE SEASON

JANUARY 2018

Monday	01	Leeds United	A	3.00pm
Saturday	**13**	**ASTON VILLA**	**H**	**3.00pm**
Saturday	20	Wolverhampton Wanderers	A	3.00pm
Saturday	**27**	**PRESTON NORTH END**	**H**	**3.00pm**

FEBRUARY 2018

Saturday	03	Fulham	A	3.00pm
Saturday	**10**	**HULL CITY**	**H**	**3.00pm**
Saturday	17	Burton Albion	A	3.00pm
Tuesday	**20**	**READING**	**H**	**7.45pm**
Saturday	24	Queens Park Rangers	A	3.00pm

MARCH 2018

Saturday	**03**	**BIRMINGHAM CITY**	**H**	**3.00pm**
Tuesday	06	Norwich City	A	7.45pm
Saturday	**10**	**DERBY COUNTY**	**H**	**1.00pm**
Saturday	17	Sheffield United	A	3.00pm
Friday	30	Millwall	A	3.00pm

APRIL 2018

Monday	**02**	**BARNSLEY**	**H**	**3.00pm**
Saturday	07	Middlesbrough	A	3.00pm
Tuesday	**10**	**BRENTFORD**	**H**	**3.00pm**
Saturday	**14**	**IPSWICH TOWN**	**H**	**3.00pm**
Saturday	21	Cardiff City	A	3.00pm
Saturday	**28**	**BRISTOL CITY**	**H**	**3.00pm**

MAY 2018

Sunday	06	Bolton Wanderers	A	12.30pm

WHAT'S GOING TO HAPPEN IN 2018?

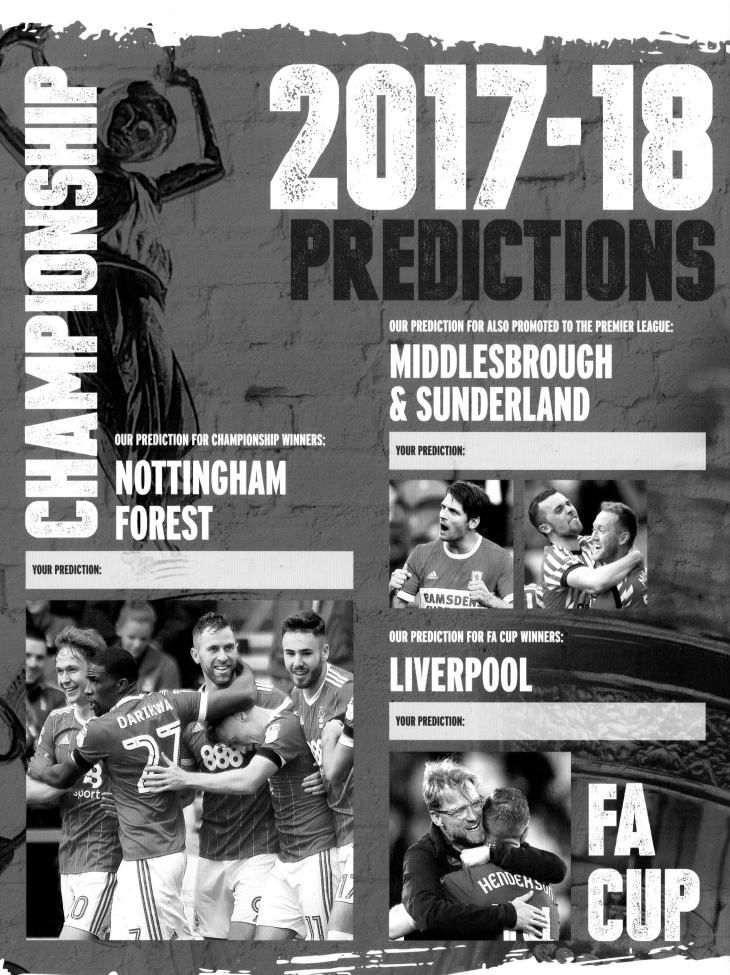

CHAMPIONSHIP

2017-18 PREDICTIONS

OUR PREDICTION FOR ALSO PROMOTED TO THE PREMIER LEAGUE:

MIDDLESBROUGH & SUNDERLAND

YOUR PREDICTION:

OUR PREDICTION FOR CHAMPIONSHIP WINNERS:

NOTTINGHAM FOREST

YOUR PREDICTION:

OUR PREDICTION FOR FA CUP WINNERS:

LIVERPOOL

YOUR PREDICTION:

FA CUP

...YOU DECIDE!

PREMIER LEAGUE

OUR PREDICTION FOR PREMIER LEAGUE CHAMPIONS:

MANCHESTER UNITED

YOUR PREDICTION:

OUR PREDICTION FOR PREMIER LEAGUE BOTTOM THREE:

WBA, STOKE CITY
NEWCASTLE UNITED

YOUR PREDICTION:

OUR PREDICTION FOR PREMIER LEAGUE RUNNERS-UP:

ARSENAL

YOUR PREDICTION:

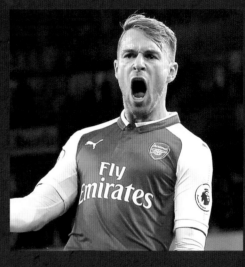

OUR PREDICTION FOR LEAGUE CUP WINNERS:

CHELSEA

YOUR PREDICTION:

LEAGUE CUP

ANSWERS

FOREST ★★

PAGE 33 · FOOTBALL 50

The missing word is FIXTURE

PAGE 38 · THE CHAMPIONSHIP CHALLENGE

1. John Terry. 2. Bayern Munich. 3. Steve Bruce. 4. Angus MacDonald. 5. Crystal Palace.
6. Paul Heckingbottom. 7. Craig Gardner. 8. 2011. 9. Jota. 10. Four times.
11. Middlesbrough. 12. Phil Parkinson. 13. 4-1. 14. Neal Maupay. 15. Mark Warburton.
16. Tammy Abraham. 17. Watford. 18. Tammy Abraham. 19. Nigel Clough. 20. Liam Boyce.
21. Stephen Warnock. 22. Red. 23. Neil Warnock. 24. Gary Medel. 25. Bradley Johnson.
26. 1946. 27. Tom Huddlestone. 28. Atletico Madrid. 29. Marcus Bettinelli.
30. Tom Cairney. 31. The Tigers. 32. Russia. 33. Arsenal. 34. Joe Garner.
35. Sir Alf Ramsey. 36. 1977-78. 37. Marching On Together. 38. Seven. 39. Liam Cooper.
40. Connor Roberts. 41. Seville, 42. The League Cup. 43. Neil Harris.
44. Manchester United. 45. The Lions. 46. Borussia Dortmund II. 47. Four.
48. Angus Gunn. 49. Newcastle United. 50. True. 51. Liam Bridcutt. 52. Jordan Hugill.
53. David Moyes. 54. Won all four divisions of English football. 55. Nedum Onuoha.
56. Christopher Samba. 57. Martin O'Neill. 58. Jaap Stam,. 59. Third. 60. Vito Mannone.
61. Leon Clarke. 62. 100. 63. Chelsea. 64. George Boyd.
65. 150 years old, they were formed in 1867. 66. 8. 67. Callum McManaman.
68. Three: Aston Villa, Preston North End and Leeds United.
69. George Honeyman and Lynden Gooch. 70. Southampton. 71. Six. 72. Ruben Neves.

PAGE 44 · WHAT BALL?

A. Ball 1. B. Ball 6.

PAGE 50 · WORLD CUP QUIZ

1930. Argentina. 1930. Argentina. 1934. Four. 1938. Paris. 1950. USA.
1954. Hungary. 1958 & 1962. Brazil. 1966. World Cup Willie. 1970. Italy.
1974. The Cruyff turn, after legendary Dutch footballer Johan Cruyff. 1978. Mario Kempes.
1982. Peter Shilton. 1986. Diego Maradona. 1990. Steve Hodge. 1994. Russia.
1998. Ronaldo. 2002. Miroslav Klose. 2006. Portugal 1-0 Netherlands.
2010. New Zealand. They drew all three of the games.
2014. Hosts: Brazil. Winners: Germany. 2018. Russia.

PAGE 52 · FAN'TASTIC ▶

PAGE 56 · HOME TURF

1. West Bromwich Albion, The Hawthorns, 26,852.
2. Birmingham City, St Andrew's Stadium, 29,409.
3. Everton, Goodison Park, 39,572.
4. Arsenal, Emirates Stadium, 60,432.
5. Manchester United, Old Trafford, 75,643.
6. Aston Villa, Villa Park, 42,682.
7. Queens Park Rangers, Loftus Road, 18,439.
8. Sunderland, Stadium of Light, 49,000.
9. Leicester City, King Power Stadium, 32,312.
10. Ipswich Town, Portman Road, 30,311.
11. West Ham United, London Stadium, 57,000.
12. Fulham, Craven Cottage, 25,700.
13. Burnley, Turf Moor, 21,800.
14. Southampton, St Mary's Stadium, 32,505.
15. Stoke City, bet365 Stadium, 27,902.
16. Norwich City, Carrow Road, 27,244.
17. Wolverhampton Wanderers, Molineux Stadium, 31,700.
18. Millwall, The Den, 20,146.
19. Chelsea, Stamford Bridge, 41,663.
20. Derby County, Pride Park Stadium, 33,597.